RARE MASTERPIECES OF RUSSIAN PIANO MUSIC

Eleven Pieces by
Glinka, Balakirev, Glazunov
and Others

Edited by Dmitry Feofanov

School of Music
University of Kentucky

DOVER PUBLICATIONS, INC.
New York

ACKNOWLEDGMENTS

The Editor wishes to acknowledge those friends and colleagues from the University of Kentucky whose help was essential in completing this project: Dr. Joe B. Buttram, Dr. Arthur Graham, Mr. Allan Ho and Mr. Benny Arnold.

The contributions of Carol Sampson are too many to enumerate.

Special thanks are also due to Victor Pavlovich Frayonov of the Moscow Conservatory, whose interest in and dedication to Russian music left a profound impression on us, his students.

This Dover edition, first published in 1984, is a republication of the complete editions of A. Liadov, *Preliudiia, si-minor, dlia fortepiano* [*Prelude in C Minor for Piano*], originally published by Gosudarstvennoe Muzykal'noe Izdatel'stvo [State Music Publishing House], Moscow and Leningrad, 1950; and of Glinka, *Tiazhely mne dumy (Molitva)* [*My Thoughts Are Heavy (Prayer)*], originally published by Gosudarstvennoe Muzykal'noe Izdatel'stvo [State Music Publishing House], Moscow and Leningrad, 1950; and of selections from the following editions:

From Balakirev, *Polnoe sobranie sochineniĭ dlia fortep'iano*, t. I, ch. I [*Complete Collected Works for Piano*, vol. I, part I], originally published by Gosudarstvennoe Muzykal'noe Izdatel'stvo [State Music Publishing House], Moscow and Leningrad, 1951: Rêverie.

From Liapunov, *Dvenadtsat' ètiudov* [*Twelve Etudes*], originally published by Gosudarstvennoe Muzykal'noe Izdatel'stvo [State Music Publishing House], Moscow and Leningrad, 1974: Transcendental Etude, Op. 11, No. 10.

From Medtner, *Sobranie sochineniĭ*, t. II: *Sochineniia dlia fortep'iano* [*Collected Works*, vol. II: *Compositions for Piano*], originally published by Gosudarstvennoe Muzykal'noe Izdatel'stvo [State Music Publishing House], Moscow, 1959: Sonata, Op. 22.

From *Al'bom fortep'ianykh p'es*, vypusk vtoroĭ [*Album of Piano Pieces*, second edition (title also given in Azerbaijani)], edited by Ikinchi Barakhylysh, originally published by Azerbaĭdzhanskoe Gosudarstvennoe Muzykal'noe Izdatel'stvo [Azerbaijan State Music Publishing House], Baku, 1962: Griboedov (Griboyedov), Two Waltzes, and Kalinnikov, Nocturne in F-sharp Minor.

From *Etiudy konkursnye* [*Etudes for Competitions*], edited by E. Khoven, originally published by Izdatel'stvo "Muzyka" ["Music" Publishing House], Moscow, 1971: Schlözer, Etude in A-flat Major.

From *Polifonicheskie p'esy russkikh kompozitorov* [*Polyphonic Pieces by Russian Composers*], edited by V. Natanson, originally published by Izdatel'stvo "Muzyka" ["Music" Publishing House], Moscow, 1971: Glazunov, Prelude and Fugue in D Minor, and Taneev (Taneyev), Prelude and Fugue, Op. 29.

From *Sbornik starinnykh sonat dlia fortep'iano* [*Collection of Early Sonatas for Piano*], edited by E. Bekman-Shcherbina and M. Ivanov-Beretskiĭ, originally published by Gosudarstvennoe Muzykal'noe Izdatel'stvo [State Music Publishing House], Moscow, 1959: Hässler, Sonata-Fantasie, Op. 4.

Manufactured in the United States of America
Dover Publications, Inc.
31 East 2nd Street, Mineola, N.Y. 11501

Library of Congress Cataloging in Publication Data
Main entry under title:

Rare masterpieces of Russian piano music.

Reprinted from editions published in the Soviet Union, 1950–1974.
Contents: Reverie / Balakirev—Prelude & Fugue / Glazunov—Prayer / Glinka—[etc.]
1. Piano music. 2. Music—Soviet Union. I. Glinka, Mikhail Ivanovich, 1804–1857. II. Feofanov, Dmitry.
M21.R26 1984   83-20521
ISBN 0-486-24659-0

CONTENTS

INTRODUCTION

The blossoming of Russian musical art during the late nineteenth and early twentieth centuries has few parallels in the history of music. A country which during the early decades of the nineteenth century produced little more than amateurish aping of Western musical styles, Russia in less than fifty years became the home of one of the world's major musical cultures. Mussorgsky, Tchaikovsky, Scriabin, Rachmaninov, Prokofiev and Schostakovich—giants in the annals of music—were nurtured in this culture.

Alongside these titans were numerous composers who, had they had the fortune (or misfortune?) of being born elsewhere, would now have the title of "the Father of Such-and-Such Music" bestowed upon them. In the volcanic artistic atmosphere of their own era they were sometimes completely overshadowed, and became known only to an elite circle of music historians, a fate ill-deserved by their fine talents.

This volume is an attempt to begin remedying the wrong, by presenting a sampling of little-known Russian piano music from the late eighteenth to early twentieth centuries. In their struggle for a national style, Russian composers concentrated primarily on opera, sadly neglecting piano music (except for Tchaikovsky and Scriabin). Along the way, however, some of them enriched the piano repertoire with first-class works which deserve to be known and performed. The music included here is intended primarily for performance, but should also be of interest to music historians, since most of it is out of print. Musical worth was the principal consideration in selecting the works; other factors considered were the unfamiliarity of a composer or composition and the historical value of the work.

BALAKIREV, MILY ALEKSEYEVICH
(1837–1910)

Russian composer, pianist, music educator, spiritual leader of the "Mighty Band" (commonly and mistakenly referred to as "The Five"). Balakirev's role in the development of the Russian Nationalist School is difficult to overemphasize. Himself a highly gifted composer with a certain "catalytic" quality, he directed his energies toward fostering the projects of disciples and friends. Without him we would not have Tchaikovsky's *Romeo and Juliet* and *Manfred*, Rimsky-Korsakov's *The Maid of Pskov* and *Antar*, Borodin's symphonies and, to a lesser degree, Mussorgsky's *Boris Godunov*. After a period of intense musical activity and rivalry with the musical establishment of the 1860s (with the activities of the Free Music School as a focal point), Balakirev turned away from music, took a civil service job and became fanatically religious. Returning to active composition in the mid-1890s, he produced a quantity of works, most of which are inferior to his earlier achievements.

"Rêverie" is a late work that is characteristic of Balakirev at his best. An affinity with Chopin and Liszt is apparent in the piano texture and harmony, while the melody's Oriental flavor conjures up *Scheherazade*. Architectonically, "Rêverie" is a masterpiece—a synthesis of a three-part and sonata form, in which, after a dramatic development of thematic ideas, the dream vanishes in a coda of almost impressionistic tone-painting. An adventurous pianist will not miss the chance to pair this rarely performed piece with another late Balakirev gem, the Scherzo in B-flat Minor, available in another Dover volume, *Nineteenth-Century European Piano Music* (John Gillespie, editor, 1976, 23447-9).

GLAZUNOV, ALEKSANDR KONSTANTINOVICH
(1865–1936)

Russian composer, pupil of Rimsky-Korsakov, member of the "Beliayev Circle" (a spin-off of the "Mighty Band"). As director of the St. Petersburg (later Leningrad) Conservatory for almost a quarter of a century, Glazunov had a profound influence on Russian musical life. His persistent fight against state-sponsored anti-Semitism and his well-known liberal views brought him the respect of the entire Russian musical community. Hardly a musician existed in Russia in whose life Glazunov did not play some sort of decisive role. Of his numerous students, Glazunov literally saved the life of the most famous, Schostakovich,* by insisting that he receive a special food allowance during the Civil War famine. Schostakovich later remembered Glazunov fondly in *Testimony*, his memoirs, recently smuggled out of the Soviet Union.

Highly respected as a composer, Glazunov was noted for his superb compositional technique (sometimes on the borderline of academicism) and his amazing memory, one of the most incredible manifestations of which was his restoration of the Overture and Third Act of *Prince Igor* after Borodin's death.

---

*This spelling of his name was affirmed by the composer's musical signature in the Tenth Symphony and Eighth Quartet.

Glazunov's piano music includes two outstanding piano sonatas (a genre well suited to his epic genius), numerous miniatures, several preludes and fugues and two concerti, all displaying his fine craftsmanship and nobility of thought.

The Prelude and Fugue in D Minor included here was written in 1899, when Glazunov was at the height of his creative powers. This majestic work is symphonic in concept: the baroque-inspired prelude is followed by a triple fugue in which contrapuntal activity is gradually replaced with dramatic motive development, climaxing with the return of the prelude theme in combination with the first fugue subject, followed by a broad chordal conclusion.

GLINKA, MIKHAIL IVANOVICH
(1804–1857)

Russian nationalist composer, "the Father of Russian Music." Primarily known for his two operas, *A Life for the Tsar* (also known as *Ivan Susanin*), and *Ruslan and Lyudmila*, which established epic and fairy-tale operas as basic avenues of Russian operatic art. Glinka wrote a number of piano pieces in styles ranging from cheap virtuosity (a result of Italian operatic influences) to one of a more sincere tenor, approaching Chopin.

"Prayer," a mildly programmatic piece (considering the epigraph taken from the nineteenth-century Russian lyric poet Aleksey Kol'tsov), was written in 1847 and transcribed for chorus and orchestra in 1855. The vocally influenced themes are integrated into an exquisitely individualized musical form (Introduction A B A^I B^I A^{II}, where A^{II} also serves as a coda). Glinka had a special emotional attachment to this piece. In a letter to a friend he wrote: "This prayer departed with a scream from my soul in 1847 in Smolensk during a terrible nervous suffering."

Instrumental compositions unfortunately were not Glinka's most important contribution to the development of Russian music; his operas and orchestral pieces, however, summed up previous attempts to create a national opera and laid the foundations for a mature Russian musical style of world importance. This "focal" quality in Glinka's oeuvre lends even relatively insignificant pieces like "Prayer" a certain consequence.

GRIBOYEDOV, ALEKSANDR SERGEYEVICH
(1795–1829)

Russian playwright, diplomat and amateur composer, Griboyedov was immortalized by his comedy *Woe from Wit*, in Russia considered to be on a par with some of Pushkin's masterpieces. He did not receive a systematic musical education (a trait shared by many nineteenth-century Russian composers, including the greatest of them, Mussorgsky), but a certain degree of musical proficiency was expected from members of the Russian nobility before the age of hi-fi.

Griboyedov and his staff of thirty-six were massacred while on diplomatic assignment in Teheran, when a crowd of a hundred thousand, encouraged by mullahs, stormed the Russian embassy (the mullahs haven't changed much, it seems). As an apology, the Shah of Iran sent a magnificent diamond to Nicholas II. This diamond, called "The Shah," is today on permanent display in the Kremlin along with other treasures of the Russian tsars.

The two waltzes included in this volume are still quite popular in Russia, and are used primarily as pedagogical repertoire.

HÄSSLER, JOHANN WILHELM
(1747–1822)

Russian composer of German birth. Hässler was one of a number of foreign musicians who made their homes in Russia. After completing a number of compositions in his native Germany, he underscored the turning point in his career by beginning anew with Opus 1 upon arrival in Russia. He is best remembered by historians of music for his keyboard contest with Mozart, which Hässler lost. Although it is doubtful that he stood much of a chance, the very fact of this competition indicates he was held in high esteem and considered a worthy competitor in German musical circles.

The Sonata-Fantasie, Op. 4, comes from the year 1795, shortly after Hässler settled in St. Petersburg. A delightful and energetic piece, the Fantasie's musical language is surprisingly operatic: instrumental and aria-like movements alternate with secco and accompanied recitatives, in the tradition of C. P. E. Bach and anticipating Beethoven.

KALINNIKOV, VASILY SERGEYEVICH
(1866–1901)

Russian composer and conductor. Kalinnikov's tragic death from tuberculosis came at the very time his fresh and sincere talent was on the verge of crossing the line that separates amateur from professional. His most successful work, the Symphony in G Minor, displays the most attractive features of Kalinnikov's style: broad, characteristically national melodic lines, advanced chromatic harmony and naïve simplicity. Some defects are also present—the quality of the material is not consistent, developmental technique is lacking and transitional episodes are often weak. Despite all this, the Symphony remains a beloved part of the orchestral repertoire in Russia.

The Nocturne in F-sharp Minor was written in 1894. Had Kalinnikov lived longer, he might well have become a major figure in Russian music, or so we can deduce from analyzing this score. The lush harmonies, well-defined melodic lines using inexact sequencing and refined piano texture full of chromatic inner voices all suggest an affinity with Tchaikovsky and early Scriabin (1890s on).

Western musicology has yet to do a comprehensive study on this highly original composer. It appears that no significant research projects on Kalinnikov have been undertaken as of this date.

LIADOV, ANATOLY KONSTANTINOVICH
(1855–1914)

Russian composer-miniaturist. As a professor at the Moscow Conservatory, Liadov was instrumental in educating the next generation of composers, most notably Miaskovsky and Prokofiev. In the case of the latter, his influence is clear to anyone who takes the trouble to compare the *Visions Fugitives* with Liadov's miniatures. Attention to detail, precision of execution, fairy-tale atmosphere—all of this in Prokofiev's works undoubtedly comes from Liadov. Moreover, Liadov, despite his avowed conservatism, may have unwillingly encouraged Prokofiev's musical experimentation, for he himself was not immune to the spirit of the times, especially in his orchestral mood-pictures. The augmented chords and unresolved dominants which were later labeled "Scriabinisms" are already present in Liadov's music of years earlier.

Unfortunately, this incredibly gifted musician had one flaw: he was notoriously lazy. In this he managed to give a helping hand to another up-and-coming Russian musician—Stravinsky. It was Liadov who was commissioned to compose the *Firebird*, and who made the inquiring Diaghilev blow up and transfer the commission to Stravinsky several weeks before the premiere by telling him that the music paper had already been bought.

Piano music occupies a central place in Liadov's output. Though known primarily for the delightful *Musical Snuff-Box*, he produced over forty works of highly refined piano music. The Prelude included here is a worthy example of Liadov's art: painstakingly crafted, it is reminiscent of Chopin in its harmonic smoothness and of Rachmaninov in its broad melodic lines.

LIAPUNOV, SERGEY MIKHAILOVICH
(1859–1924)

Russian composer and pianist. He studied piano with Klindworth and Pabst, composition with Tchaikovsky and Taneyev. Upon graduation from the Moscow Conservatory he became closely associated with Balakirev, to the point of subjecting his own creative will to Balakirev's and becoming his faithful follower. Having accepted Balakirev as his musical messiah, Liapunov inevitably fell under the spell of one of Balakirev's idols, Liszt, and became an ardent champion of the great Hungarian master. This led to the appearance of one of the most interesting phenomena in Russian piano music: twelve Transcendental Etudes, Op. 11, No. 10 of which is included here. The Etudes are dedicated to the memory of Liszt, and complete the key sequence of Liszt's own Transcendental Etudes.

All of the Etudes make ample use of Lisztian technique; some are openly modeled after Liszt's originals. The subtitle of the one included is "Lezginka," the name of a fast, impetuous folk dance of Dagestan, an area in the Caucasus. This makes it a double tribute: in addition to Liszt, a reference to Balakirev and his "Oriental Fantasy," *Islamey*, is clearly intended.

"Lezginka" is technically easier than *Islamey* but no less effective. The resources of the piano are explored fully and idiomatically, no doubt thanks to Liapunov's own outstanding pianistic prowess. Particularly striking is the thematic material, which anticipates later twentieth-century experiments with non-Western modes and sonorities.

MEDTNER, NIKOLAY KARLOVICH
(1880–1951)

Russian composer and pianist of German descent. Philosopher as well as musician, Medtner was a spiritual descendant of the German idealist philosophers. His duality of heritage led him to complement his idealism with strong ethical convictions derived from Russian Orthodoxy. A true and staunch conservative in art, he created an individual style of considerable originality which encompasses certain modernistic tendencies, but is in essence firmly based on classical foundations. (Medtner, incidentally, belongs to that elite breed of composers whose styles are fully formed from the very beginning of their creative careers.) The name of the treatise setting forth his musical credo is characteristic: *The Muse and Fashion: In Defense of the Foundations of Musical Art*.

Though chiefly remembered for his *Fairy Tales*, Medtner enriched the piano repertoire with some twelve sonatas, of which Op. 22, Op. 25, No. 2, Op. 38 ("Reminiscenza"), Op. 39 ("Tragica") and Op. 53, No. 2 ("Minacciosa") are most notable. The Sonata in G Minor, Op. 22, the third of Medtner's sonatas, is an outstanding example of Medtner's masterly treatment of thematic development and form and of his demanding piano style. These features, derived from the German Romantic tradition, prove him to be a direct musical descendant of Beethoven and Brahms.

SCHLÖZER, PYOTR (PAUL) VON
(1841–1898)

Russian pianist and composer of German descent. Very little is known of Schlözer's life, except for his professorship at the Moscow Conservatory (his most important student is discussed below) and his authorship of Two Etudes, Op. 1, the more famous of which is included here. (Another important historical fact: his niece, Tatyana, became Scriabin's second wife.) All attempts to pin down this phantom composer further proved inconclusive. In the absence of hard facts one is left to rely on two legends: first, that the etudes that made Schlözer famous were really written by the well-known Polish composer Moritz Moszkowski, who lost them to Schlözer in a card game; and second, that Rachmaninov began his exercise routine with the A-flat Major Etude daily throughout his career.

One does become suspicious, comparing the Schlözer etude with, for instance, Moszkowski's Op. 72, No. 11 (also in A-flat Major), for the similarity is striking. On the other hand, this very similarity may have given rise to the legend. One way or another, this is an excellent encore piece—flashy, suited to the salon, beautifully written for the instrument. Melodiya disc D-031711/2 features a stunning performance by Liszt student Vera Timanova, who recorded this etude during the first decade of the century.

Schlözer's best-known student appears to have been Leonid Sabaneyev, a prominent music historian and critic whose book *Modern Russian Composers* is an indispensable and sometimes the sole source of information on many completely forgotten figures of Russian music.

TANEYEV, SERGEY IVANOVICH
(1856–1915)

Russian composer, pianist and theorist. A disciple of Tchaikovsky and N. Rubinstein, whom he succeeded as director of the Moscow Conservatory, Taneyev was the teacher of Scriabin and Rachmaninov, and indirectly, through Glière, Prokofiev. He occupies a unique position in the line of Russian composers: never before had they included a figure of Taneyev's intellectual power and a breadth of pursuit resembling the giants of the Renaissance.

Taneyev's compositions are few (thirty-six assigned opus numbers and a number of unpublished pieces), but their consistent quality is notable. Among his theoretical contributions are *Invertible Counterpart in the Strict Style* (a treatise some claim is still unsurpassed in its exploration of complex contrapuntal combinations) and *The Study of Canon*, unfortunately unfinished. Taneyev's interest in counterpoint led him to develop one of the most sophisticated and powerful compositional techniques of the century; his scientific research led him to predict the disintegration of tonality's gravitational pull and the rise of polyphony as a unifying force as early as 1906. Even the four forms of series are described in the preface to his book. Paradoxically, he was a musical conservative, deploring this development. His own musical style is marked by fiery intellectualism, precision, forcefulness, thick, often contrapuntal textures and rapid modulations to distant keys.

The Prelude and Fugue, Op. 29, is a case in point. The musical material is organized with the iron hand of a composer at the height of his creative powers. Technically, it is a tour de force of almost unsurpassed difficulty (Taneyev was a virtuoso pianist who premiered several of Tchaikovsky's piano works). One can only regret that it is Taneyev's sole piano composition and hope that some adventurous virtuoso will soon bring this truly remarkable piece to the public's attention.

RARE MASTERPIECES OF RUSSIAN PIANO MUSIC

Eleven Pieces by
Glinka, Balakirev, Glazunov
and Others

MILY BALAKIREV
Rêverie

1

poco a poco stringendo al fine

cantabile

ALEKSANDR GLAZUNOV
Prelude and Fugue in D Minor, Op. 62

Dedicated to Auguste Bernard

Fuga a due suggetti
Moderato

MIKHAIL GLINKA
Prayer ("My Thoughts Are Heavy")

Andante con molto espressione. Con abbandone ♩=98
Спокойно, очень выразительно, непринужденно

Prayer   25

Maestoso ma l'istesso movi-
Величественно, но в том же
-mento
движении

Mikhail Glinka

Maestoso ma l'isteso
Величественно, но в

movimento
том же движении

*) This and the following three measures are absent from the autograph.

*) In the autograph:

ALEKSANDR GRIBOYEDOV
Two Waltzes

Waltz in A-flat Major

Waltz in E Minor

[Allegretto]

Aleksandr Griboyedov

JOHANN HÄSSLER
Sonata-Fantasie, Op. 4

Recitativo

Recitativo

Allegro

VASILY KALINNIKOV
Nocturne in F-sharp Minor

ANATOLY LIADOV
Prelude, Op. 11, No. 1

np.p. = r. h.

SERGEY LIAPUNOV
Transcendental Etude, Op. 11, No. 10 ("Lezginka")

NIKOLAY MEDTNER
Sonata in G Minor, Op. 22 *)

Dedicated to L. Catoire

*) The eighths here a little slower (calmer) than the quarters in the *Allegro*.

*) Marcato (the thumb of the left hand only).

*) The "a" may be left on the fermata.

*) To master this rhythm one should use, in a slow tempo, the compromise indicated on the foregoing page:

PYOTR SCHLÖZER
Etude in A-flat Major, Op. 1, No. 2

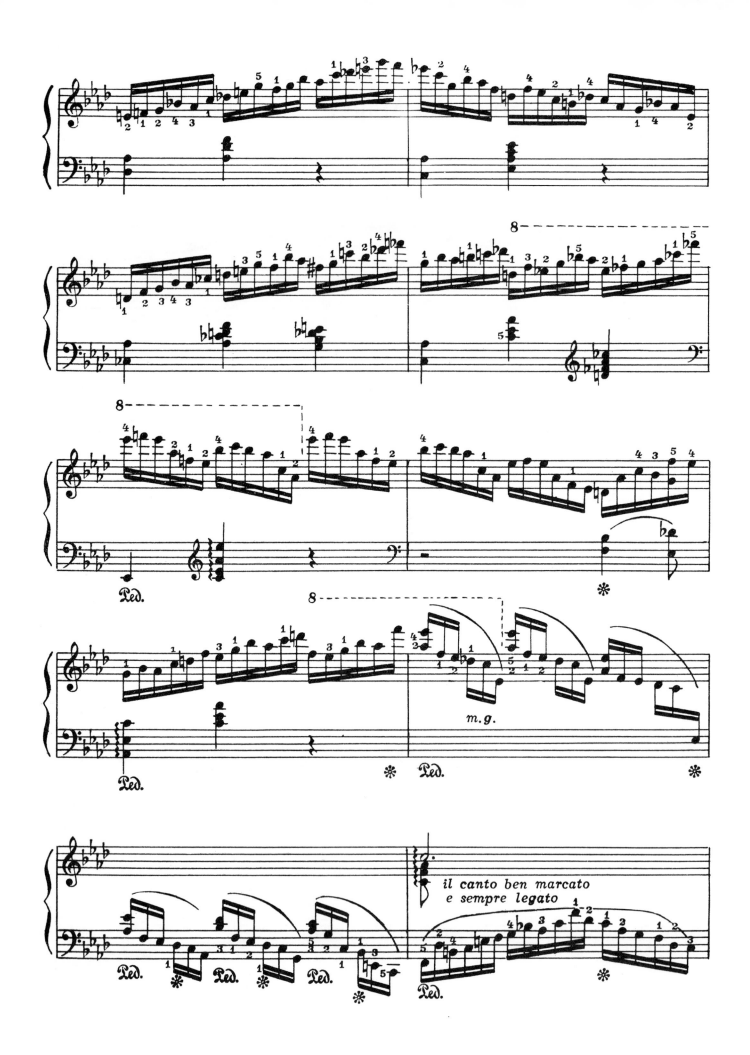

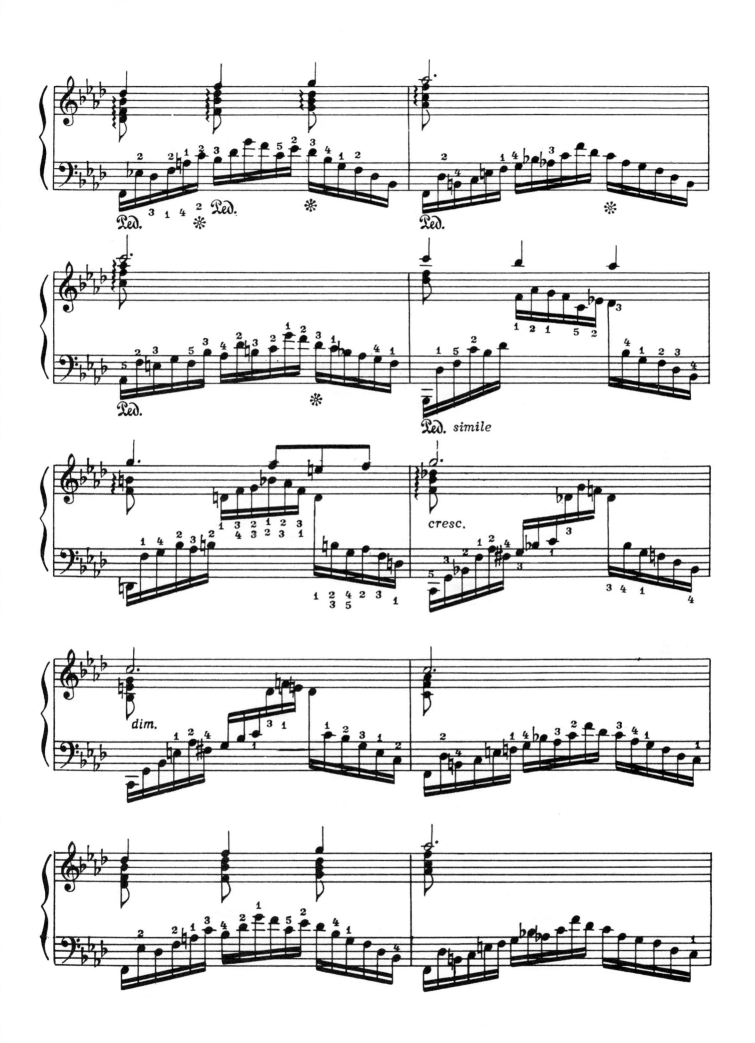

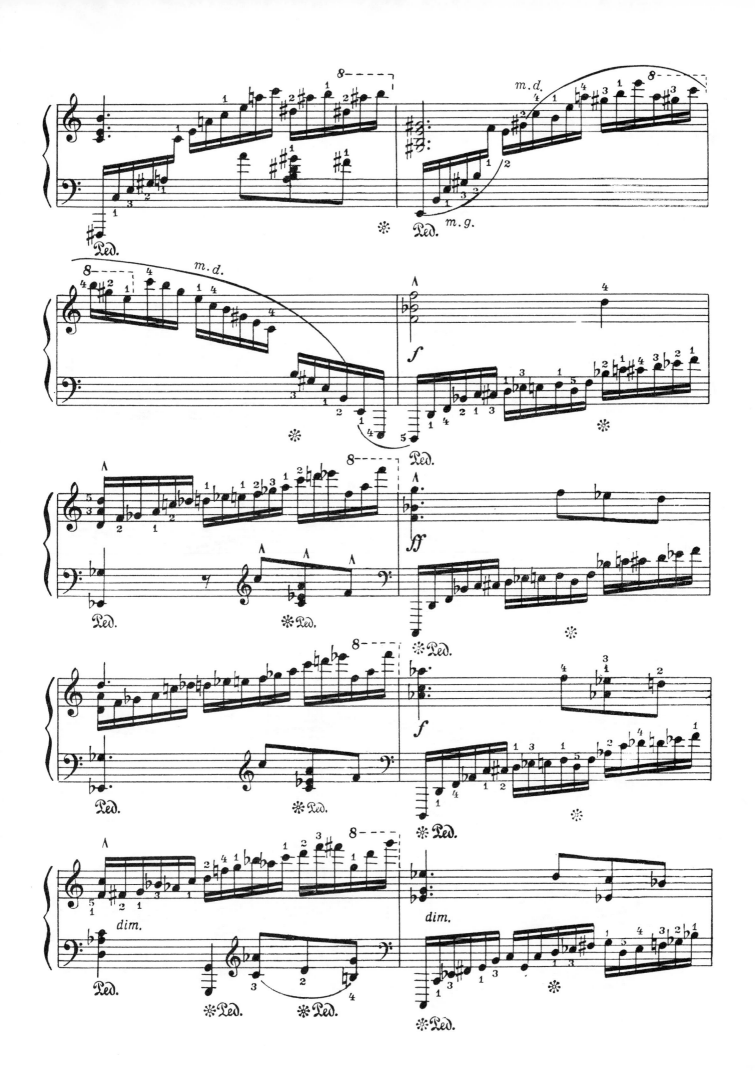

SERGEY TANEYEV
Prelude and Fugue, Op. 29

Prelude

Fugue

Allegro vivace e con fuoco